marcella durand

AREA

Text, cover design, & typesetting by HR Hegnauer.
Original cover art *purple forbidden enclosure* © Suzan Frecon.

AREA was printed in a first edition of 1000 copies by Thomson-Shore, Inc on acid free
Natures Natural, 50% post-consumer recycled paper.
Printed in the United States, 2008.

Belladonna* is a reading and publication series that promotes the work of women
writers who are adventurous, experimental, politically involved, multiform, multi-
cultural, multi-gendered, impossible to define, delicious to talk about, unpredictable,
& dangerous with language. Belladonna* is supported with funds
granted by the New York State Council on the Arts, The Fund for
Poetry, and by donations. This book was made possible by FACE OUT,
a grant program organized by the Council for Literary Magazines &
Presses with the support of The Jerome Foundation and The New York
Community Trust. The mission of
FACE OUT is to maximize the
visibility of emerging writers.

State of the Arts

NYSCA [clmp] THE NEW YORK COMMUNITY TRUST NYCT

ISBN: 978-0-9764857-5-9

Distributed to the trade by
Small Press Distribution
1341 Seventh Street
Berkeley, CA 94710
www.SPDBooks.org

Also directly available through
Belladonna Books
925 Bergen Street, Suite 405
Brooklyn, NY 11238
www.BelladonnaSeries.org

*deadly nightshade, a cardiac and respiratory stimulant, having purplish-red flowers and black berries.

AREA

marcella durand

Belladonna Books
Brooklyn, New York
2008

Table of Contents

The Spatial Dimensions of Elephant Migrations .. 3

The Orange Line .. 11

Scale Shift .. 17

Remote Sensing .. 21

The Verneuil Process .. 29

False Color View .. 37

Apparent Orbits .. 43

The Apparent Orbit .. 45
From Terra, Here .. 46
Mars, Naming War .. 47
In Jupiter .. 48
To Saturn .. 49
To Neptune .. 50

Opticks .. 51

BOX .. 53
The Formation of Opticks .. 54
The Mechanicks of Formation .. 55
botanic .. 56
"on a distant mesa, surrounded by desert" .. 57

The Anatomy of Oil .. 59

The Clocktower .. 81

Acknowledgements & Notes .. 88

About the Author .. 89

Colophon .. 90

At this point, it could become static. A seascape. Perhaps pointillist. Small colors building up to a view. The waves almost seem to lap, the sails almost billow. And close to the crater, they do. They may lap. And they may carry away crumpled candy wrappers, potato chip bags, and bits of hamburger buns. At the small beach close to the airport, people carrying a giant netted bag filled with clams assured us that the tide was clean here, coming in straight from the ocean. We saw black smoke on the horizon and heard sirens. The bus driver announced that he was skipping all stops. We had misjudged the magnitude of it, initially, and after all, if we couldn't taste it, it was hard to imagine that it was there. The bridge to this island is often unplowed. The springs and magnetism have a certain effect on cellphones, internet access, and regular phone service. No one explains it, least of all the line workers. The same cable has been down for years at the top of the hill. After the last ice storm, the weather was worried. Completely deconstructed. A black-and-white scene. No color to it at all. Only snow and wires, and giant steel structures crumpled in fascinating patterns.

it was an aggravated shape that hung on the wall
pointed, it led in every direction
it wanted to be discrete
but nailed as it was, it remained visual
like making a map with eyes shut
while traveling

two different
modes of escape
one manmade
(dirty)

The Spatial Dimensions of Elephant Migrations

A corona abuts the erosion.
Fracture lines emanate OUT.
Could be lines like any other, cavities like any other—
Are they *trying* to be bad?

Relax the regulations.
Apply the exemptions.
If you cross here, you will be retaliatorily poached, but that isn't the protest.
Perhaps you were expecting a caffeine-fueled explication
or, no, you are under investigation as of this word:

x

Your national park occurred later yesterday, the stalagmite…
a crevasse, shatter
piercing you
at center, not off.

I would have hiked there—
Would I have hiked there
or migrated away?

You found him standing in the meadow, vast.
An open sky, an eye open.
In the meadow, vastness and then
a road to which—

Strange,
to be surrounded. What is
this stone?

It wasn't the
Shape you expected. Is that break
hard enough? It is a Noun
and stands on four legs, skin
falling down around its ankles.
Grey. Time to introduce Green.

Miles of golden browns with
purple tinge. As far as—

As far as the cities. Displace it.
They weren't right
about the land-use rights. And
sold off their air zones. Cloning
didn't work. It was
not the embryo but the
being carrying it. Something
does embrace.

incompatible
tenderness

Just an uplift. A frustration. A long lean wall
in the same colors as we were trying
to describe. Then topiary.

Set off by red next to gold and red over that.
Whether a light or dark in the composition.
Fluorescent light flattening or cold. When we entered the place.
Dark stone. Unburnished.

The tips about us were turning watery and dumping themselves
into oceans. Water swirls about our ankles. We stand
as he stands, ruminative, then suddenly violent and goring.

The hallway is mirrors, but nobody seems to see. Only the
beveled window gives off small light. And, at this time of year, dimness.

That's when we carved the meadow's memory into the frames over the doors.
All the creatures we had seen. Would they respond?

If only the head could be cut off and then body activation with dark elementals
spewing over the deep woods. That would show them.

The same story cut up and arranged into a different pattern of shards.
Mouthing green leaves through a megaphone then chewing on soggy boards.
Caught in esophagus and gakking. Sitting sorry on the plastic bench.

That'll be *your* corner. Because
you thought one giant gray mammal
looked like another. But one floats and spews
and the other's tooth is in your socket. we have a place in the food chain too

It's always about pushing. Pushing back, pushing against. Pushing you. Pushing off.
Achieving more. Thinking good. And then, doing good. Good achievements, lots of them.
But we should be doing less, eating less, breathing less.

In pieces. Lowering it. Separations.

Very small—very, very small. Tiny.

Take Joe's advice and scatter flowers
through it: Peony. There!

But that doesn't prevent us from feeling warm
and small, as volcanoes blow upward and voices
are lost among creases—creases similar to those
of wrist, elbow, hip, knee, waist (all the places we bend).
Creases turn into canyons on the way downward,
dissembling into fans and into flatness.
Ranunculus! And what is that supposed to do, exactly?
Rose! Lilac? Borage… I spread fingers into a fan
and lay hand down, wrist angled up as though a cliff.
A dry one, cracking, matte. As dust is matte
in direct dry sunshine. Whether obscured in
particulates. This we could climb. If the top
were not transforming.

If the top were not transforming.
A farmyard baked in sun. Nothing grows.
Remembering not just a dream, but the feeling of a dream.
The ceiling when poked spills memories.
Objects, when tossed onto a lawn, distort.

And become themselves as baked into new forms.
Their structure disappears and turns circular.
Soft circles littering a lawn.

The angular tends toward circles. *Circles forming*

An envelope, opened, has sticks in it.

doesn't change A stick never melts. It torches like an idea or a dream.

Never becomes a gelatinous ball.

We may contain plastic, but we are not of it.

Explore grammar and the tedious words: is which from how it be?

of which it is somehow something when what it be?

somehow something which it is whether gets it—

it gets somehow from that which it

it does it unctuous it does from

from it gets comes realistic it something

sick of something it is and will

sick of it it is and will be

will be sick

is sick

is a sick

grey noun.

9

The Orange Line

"Not Yet.

Not Yet." About waiting. The orange line shines
and at some points undulates as indecision
or influenced by outside factors, wavers
and comes back to itself, asserts
itself as orange (although colorless in moonlight)
and as paint shining in angled light.
Irresistible and pointing toward
a smaller village-within-a-village and
history in the form of a speakeasy and then
theatres. If the body equals a city, not likely.   *temporary*
City is edifice, takes fissures, crumbles. The body   *- like a city*
painted upon, fissures, empties. Waiting. "Not
Yet." About waiting, then emptying. Fissure
in place of failure. The word "failure." From
whence you come failing along the block?

        From whence you come
        failing
        along the block?

O body, O city, O line taking me past
streetlamps and industry, supermarket, place
of lemons, mangos, and avocados already
remarked upon. I meet you nowhere except
the end of the block and hence the end
of the street. You loop and splatter, waver   *evasive, formless,*
like what? Like smoke? And then a splash   *no beginning*
to remind me I have not followed you anywhere,
certainly not to your end or beginning. But I did
keep with your past erasures, temporary

13

disappearances. I was glad to see
you again in front of a garden, although
slightly disappointed at the cliché.
Predictable. A line. You are after
all a line. Orange. Spiritual? Or corporeal?
Orange signals spirit, but shine indicates
body. Spirit to be located in the entirety
of the body. Not heart, not head. Toe and
phantom limb. Finger and cuticle. Eye
and ear. But if part lopped off, then what
happens to spirit? Curtailed, maimed?
Missing hand not visible in sky?
Only ominous moon stalked by
low cloud cover? The mist rising
to take the first-borns?
"Not yet, not yet." Not long
the first-borns, not yet any borns.
All is yet to be born, and what   line ≠ circle
was born is in the past
and already grown. Missing
hand here in archaic heart.

Orange line, where
are you? I lost you
for a second and already
I vanish, looking skyward.
Am I too practical? Too abstract?
Too preoccupied? But here
I am thinking about beginnings,
while you disappear down the street.
Do you cross the last avenue?

Do you come to the river? Where
are your fingerprints? Your hands?
Print again. I have no mark.
I did not sand them off, nor erase
them. I have no mark. Follow
then wait. Just a burn that
indicates a fingertip and
no whorl to follow. No ink
to dust or trace. No criminal
record, no rally, no political
activity. Just left in a field
for others to find. No spaceship,
no radiation, no radio. The signal   *can't translate*
is a color never seen on earth. Try
to imagine that. I imagined a sort
of violet. Now I would
imagine alabaster. A translucence
that is not transparent. A shine,
not gum stuck to the sidewalk.
Shine is only paint and not like
metal. Paint does not corrode. It   *doesn't destroy, it's destroyed*
disintegrates and only if it is oil.   *(by time)*
Acrylic doesn't breathe and can be
transported into space. It holds color
and doesn't let anyone in. It is solid   *live forever limitless if isolated*
and does not crumble or fissure. Acrylic   *and unchanged*
is waterproof, airproof. Travels
in space. Holds cylinders. Is a container.   *color, timeless*

No x-ray vision penetrates it. When it comes,
it comes. Arrives on the block and knocks
on the door. Leaves a note that it's been here.
Here I wait, watching a moon move in and out
of clouds, or clouds move around the moon, not
sure if they indicate a disaster or if the door
will open, if my key will work tonight. Like an eye,
except not oily and floating. Visual. Perceiving
all except itself. Does the beginning need to be redone?
Can't it just happen and then proceed? Do we need
to go back and fix it? I give up; I don't know where
you started. I only noticed when it grew dark
and you glimmered along the stoops and the projects.
When the dog was released from its chain
and stars resembled something fallen from
a giant corporeal being. Really, the eye
was drawn along yards of blocks to
become a mile and end at a river but before
that a building, low enough to establish
horizons and an image of sky. I only
define you in negatives. You are not
leading me on. Not yet, "not yet." If
you arrive along the serrated edges
of buildings or drawn across bricks,
if you only became shape
through complication of form, then
you were already there
color, nebulous
still as trail.

Scale Shift

Scale shift from bright blue-green through time to yellow-green as travel through
      yellow green as farther in scale leaves inside other leaves as travel through
from bluish tinge spreading to yellow green through time as going through observe
      coding red gold from yellow green and darker green codes observe
viburnum vivid across range optical spectrum as travel through geography and observe
      viburnum and pine dark green evergreen as spot in white, color against gray
shifting through time from start of season bluish green small and transparent unfurling
      going down scale through heat expansion bluish green to darker green unfurling
observe pine dark green fuller and wilted grows larger as travel through geography
      in full of season fuller wilted and yellowish tinge as observing through tinting
yellowish tinge in preparing for red gold gold and oaks brown as water in limits
      change as travel through geography or time as season changes red gold or brown yellow
tinge scale spectrum visible across range as travel through season changes red, brown, oak
      from blue-green unfurling travel through wilting season red-gold coding
and on ground almost purple violet tinged dark bluish season coming geography sap changes
      sap changes from full on to wilting summer heated and sap slows down
wooden rings expand & wooden circulatory system red-gold coding sap slows down
      as travel through geography as we would travel through yellow tinges changing
unfurling into gold, green, against white, gray as geography season changes
      as optical spectrum observe through travel geography time brown as water limits
as yellow surrounds and like water yellow in directions gold coded and water slows in season
      as season slows water and yellow-gold surrounding and observe as we are surrounded
as we are submerged in coding yellow-gold, red-gold, browns and dark green against white, gray
      as travel through spectrum in directions gold oak viburnum pine dark green against white, gray
and black indicating travel observation delineation travel observing on black against color spectrum red gold
      coded, bluish light green unfurling through spectrum time travel on black coded red-gold oak
viburnum vivid as travel through bluish light green unfurling into red-gold, browns, oak, pines
      as vivid against white, gray we are submerged in spectrum travel observing gold, green
through season changes vivid geography time we are submerged in spectrum surrounded coded red-gold
      in such colors, vivid against black, white, gray, we submerge observing as we would travel

Remote Sensing

If eyes receive light, then eyes are always visible. Skin is lined concentrically or scattered across gravel. Short blue wavelengths strike molecules. Predatory space is linear. Invisibility forms buoyancy. One searches out the other and ingests. So as above, below, and as below, above. Light bounces, a kind of decoy or attractant. Yellow, orange, red, or shimmering. Iridescence is caused by light fracturing along tissue, and dispersing. Shrimp see eight colors. A lustre metal white is the first work of painters, the primed painting seen by an utterly transparent animal. Position vision as far from self as possible. As blue face and scarlet feather locates us or in water. On canvas or over sand. Some blend in, others dazzle. Translucence swiftly rises.

Two lines appear on Landsat image and appear to be similar. Everything that appears similar is not necessarily related to each other. Or if they are related to one another that does not imply they are not necessarily alike. Or if they are alike they may not be related to each other or another. That one may only be similar in Landsat image and one may be a gully and the other a strip of vegetation. Or maybe a gully or ice crystals embedded below the surface features and maybe a landmass. Maybe a crest, summit, or top, with others related but smaller and receding into distance. Or maybe larger but appearing smaller and receding into distance. Maybe the primary erosion and then smaller erosions stemming from the primary erosion. If it appears blue when tinted. When tinted if it appears blue. If blue and related to another image could be misinterpreted and subsequent images discredited and presumed faults and fractures only being that. Although some and sometimes a majority. If it is only a scenario then it must be hypothesized and commented upon in a seven-band review. In seven bands, the colors appear and ripple transparently through which the landscape features can be seen clearly in their form if not necessarily their true hues. While in the rippling seven bands luminous and ephemeral, the landscape features may fracture or appear to fracture in the viewpoint of computer-generated hue. If they appear to fracture slightly or one conjectures oneself fractures or there is a black dot in one eye. If a black dot appears in one eye, then computer generation failed and mathematical precision is suspect. Only the indefinable and uncountable seven bands and non-definable luminosity colors in viewpoint steady. Today we know to be careful and use field investigations. We are especially adept at highlighting false linears.

The false color view appears to have been taken through three filters in line with blue, green, and methane gas. It could indicate something was untoward when at the time of the pinhole photograph the truck was parked with doors aimed at beach and small aperture allowed slow light. Doors open and sun streams in through seven band review: silver, gelatin, chlorophyll, haze brightness, bright red, lustre, and one great white eye near bottom of disk. Color added to the circumference of the gaseous body contrasts with the dimmer color of the interior. Says retoucher: "passes through a large quantity of fungiform bolted anaglyph." The south polar cap appears black, but in the misty nebulousness of the antarctic spring day, it's more a worn grey, scratched and dim like an old nickel. A rotating false color view. A Rotating False Color View. And you rub your eyes thinking such shades could never be. They could never appear except as transfused through wire and socket, cord, outlet, oil, coal, and a little water and wind.

Red floats in water, or measures thickness of acidity by refraction of false blue. Not a true blue, edging sky, but one applied in thick impasto, layer after layer, grid by grid. As a face emerges in an automated identification program, the last to appear are eyes: *as the most visible*. It takes opacity to capture light. The *tapetum lucidum* at the end of the eyes is the most reflective object. In translucency it appears dark. At the end of the eye, the retina amplifies light. At the end of vision, another you, me, more phosphorescence, shimmering in a trail we made moving through space.

Some are rectangular, others uneven. Irregular blue patches line stream channels. Risky to photograph this close to a rapidly changing fracture. That is, it complains as we stand in the middle and observe. Soon one leg will be in one place and the other will be on another landmass altogether. They document it from space. Three satellites follow each other rapidly on a slow, clear night. Again, identify urban areas from street patterns. One is bright green and the other is a mild, muted brownish-gray. One is overlaid over the other, or one came first, but which is linear and what expands in crumbling starfish shape? Tonight, the light over the chemical plants is exquisite. Long factory shadows spread over the invasive fountain grasses, pale beige heads nodding over the shallow waters.

The Verneuil Process

Not a true automatic sky, but a good enough beginning of icy cirrus clouds. They stretch across the bay and over to the other side where real ocean begins at acute angle. Go to observing the weather. It takes opacity to capture light. At the end of eye, a crenellated perception. Along lateral lines it moves via flapping and sinking to central water column. And there grows very quiet until passing giant crunching turbine and hopeful bait. Then thrashing in elevator and light fracturing along tissue.

A thin metal cast is placed over the wooden frame of the old building. It conducts fire from one railing to the next, and later, a porcelain sink will have been stained. The wall is cool and smooth to the hand and traces of the former hallway are seen on the floor. One kind of paint over another and in between a conglutinated mess of colors. Often the words you make up are the actual words you've been looking for in that 200-pound novel you call the dictionary. Or maybe it's a few loose sheets of a notebook detailing the design of the carburator you saw on the sidewalk a few chilly days ago. From perception to memory to expression, and back again. Like vibrations along the interior ribbings of a pre-cast material.

If they are seen clearly in their form then advance warning. Advance warning expires when insubstantial building materials. When insubstantial building materials shoddy quiver dreck. Shoddy quiver dreck it impacts here in my park. My park is concentric and most gentle green when most needed. My park is the center of attention and keeps out expiring styrofoam lined with concrete. It is gray lined and gentle green inside. If it felt and across miles it is felt and on calm sailboat pond. It is felt here and set off alarms here in gentle green protected park. Within my park always protected and underneath solid granite core. If you don't believe me come see outcroppings. If you don't believe me then see small needles breathe and shoddy quiver dreck, touched by. If felt by this. If across it feels and sees.

Not a true automatic sky, but the next blue phrase goes inert. Satellites and spacecraft edge across dark expanse of tongue. The air formations they create: slow erosion from head to tail with small crystalline detours. Remote sensing is as distant as a stalagmite forming or how a ruby is made. Nine on the Mohs scale and very close to diamond, even deeply colored fancy ones. A dark triangle appears in each cut tourmaline. The Umbu River Valley Mine is in far northeastern Tanzania. See through large hexagonal gem. See through ruby to you.

Giant silvery plastic waves against silver sky and silver light gleams down rock and metal canyon. It indicates ocean but is not quite actually there. A manufactured gesture to opening and tall plastic shields building renovation, useful but becomes animated interaction, function but becomes light-catalyzed form, paralyzing in conjunction of similar color with almost-natural sky: a sky forced into being by emanation of puff smoke from tall stack or small pipe at back of transportation. It will give of itself in pieces until taken down; it is unintentional and to vision, appears as close to given.

False Color View

it is the desire to push through curtains of vowels and find behind that veil the sound of
a streetlight shining blankly down a recently renovated street—like that a street could be "renovated"
and not torn up with dust and noise for every inhabitant and it always happens in front of school
each day the same view into another window, a classroom with views partially, but not totally, obscured
by construction-paper cut-outs repetitive in their blunt scissor snipping of corners and folds
perhaps orange, maybe pink, receiving through the first layer the blunt scissor
like such an instrument could find the precision of repetition, like vowels would not fall aside
or break apart when given small scissors more "dangerous" when they break in the hand

it's that desire to see parts of paper fall to the floor, more poignant in their litter than another letter
poised in the mailbox   waiting for a recipient   or a letter opener, the slightly thick steel tip too large
to fit the seam between glue and reader and you, you appear again from behind the curtain
"an old trick I shouldn't have fell for it"   like most private dicks would suspect the lump
behind the green velvet curtain, not like bright orange snowflakes, each one exactly alike,
in roadblocks and all the construction   sidewalk ripped up to reveal engines of metal
flakes of waterpipe a small green glass and keyring   display cases show a progression of coffeepots
like people crawling over a façade and endless scaffolding unrestricted and stackable   the street here with a
tower viewpoint perspective blocked by an edifice of brick   a dent in the succession of letters   unspacious and
recipients   with the regularity of correspondence arriving   contracted in that consonant way

first covered in bolts   each one unscrews to reveal a small cat calico with black and orange back
then more orange around its eyes, eight times larger than a human eye would be if set in a cat's face,
or a human eye would be one-eighth the size if set in a human face, or do I mean a cat face, like
if this cat were human, then overpopulation of recipients would be a problem, or already is
which is why it's in front of a school, covered with construction and projects, why the machine

was invented, so out of each alcove could pop a repetition and a snowflake exactly like another. A fan installed with blowers moves air filled with carbon monoxide over the river to dissolve into the mouths of migrating striped bass, making it to the dinner tables of east river fishermen.
Similar to the mustard-seed oil extraction industry in that someone was adding solvents without asking. Like a vowel hiding behind a milk-crate, or another cross-hatch at the gridlock. Industries only allow that sort of thing if you donate a very small door

filled with a small cat, who sways as if doing a kind of dance and then leaps into your files. It crawls up the metal cabinets and leans into the narrow parallel spaces left by having to be somewhere on time. It peers as you would if you had 7/8th larger size eyes into the shelf-like storage convection space. The internal drive sticks out a little awkwardly. It was green once and is now converted into a heavy angle. It's a bit of plastic not meant to be where it is, that is, lodged in your fleshy organ. You are a sculpture "made from every single bone in the human body." Located on the third floor of the museum, you "recline nonchalantly" against the other dumpster because there is an implication not fully explained in the explicatory text. There's won't be any confusion next time. If I so wish, I can listen to you on tape, but you'll never play on a *cassette recorder*. Rather you've got something inside that's only ascertained by fragments of shepherds taking grains of sheep up the eastern steppes. From there it continues up a ladder of tiny stones and then to the windowscreen, which it promptly tears out in search of swallowed greenery and a tone that no one else can duplicate. It's a wail of consonants, lifted out from beyond the moho disjunction of the first   level of an urban substratum.

From here, ultrasound changes tone as it passes through levels of boat timber discarded by the first wave of exploitation engineers. A giant figure exported to a land of philosophers. At the docks, it waits for soft bags to mildew while they say no to the unwanted patent duplication and the strange weakness in the fingers. No to the border and the magazines. No to the duplicates sent in lieu of ourselves and the unwanted representations. For us they are mirror-opposites and disregard our dictums. No to that. We raise our left hand as they raise their right to wave it all in, the money they get before us first. A giant figure in a capital city of a maze of windows. A giant rivet of masticated letters which it tears out in search of swallowed greenery and the ability to stop things before they start. A tiny stamped seed and another. Spreads like pollen. The tender shape of a vase, each side rises and arabesques, meeting at the top in a *flute mouth*. From there the letters fall out of the community system of cisterns. And you again, still the lump behind the green velvet curtain. And the cat tearing out the screen in search of swallowed greenery, in a tone putting to rest any stray consonants. Like you and me, not opposites and not reflections, makes links like runaway vowels. To be wary means discovering the drippy spring underneath the flat rock. Wouldn't you like to know where it goes? As it comes out of the rock it did come from somewhere. It's running on even through the metal and the green mosses. Count twenty

and come home over the steppes and the mountains. Close the doors and adjust the rivets. Like that a framework can be invisible. How easily one slips into this, a green velvet file cabinet and a face observing as it is observed. There's only one way language can be awkward about an arrangement. Like how we look at them, they look at us. It meant that astronomers can *see*. It's fast-moving or hasn't been filmed yet. It's a way to be more lyrical about cell division. It's a *false-color view of the scene.* A cloud of constructed sentences   circling a dense knot of stars   parsed by infra-red rays or more insecurity. The world wavers about one. Green represents firing jets. Polycyclic aromatic compounds depicted in purple. The center of the plant *is really* dark reddish brown. I daub umber on the watercolor tablet. The seafronds *took place* and were not filmed.   They were there and we did not see it. With only rays, green strikes us in such unexpected ways.   it's that the tone changes and   its range becomes that of place,   house, about and around numbers here   make up a sequence of secrets   can I know what comprises the underneath of a dwelling?   we thought a *fucus buccinali*s or a *plantarum nepalensium* a nature that drew itself or is ready to grow onto the next construction we gave it   a *botanograph* in line with that it was before a *photogene* taken without camera or lens   the object interacted with what you gave it

pressed into the book and closed   from nature's self-imprint   we helped a little with color

I daub *caput mortuum* on the watercolor tablet   the calico pattern shifts according

to events during the mother's pregnancy   cloned or not cloned   elected or not elected

        the knockoffs of the handbags inspire the handbags   from central point in pyramidal bulb,

lines radiate in not quite a circle   it is a mollusk and not, like we thought, a gilled fish

or a plant, a *lycopodium squarrosum*   from nature's self-imprint   a pattern on my arm

like to mention *laminaria fascia*, *digitata*, and again, *fascia*   vowels and consonants depicted by

cutters of construction paper and users of blunt scissors, or scaffold-builders and not exporters of damp

bags to lands of philosophers.   Declare beautiful the isolated object-planet on the fringes of

uncolored ocean and maybe part of a greater cloud of lines radiating out in not quite a circle a given

proportion lovely to the eye whether one eighth or set in the face as a planet is set in a invisible cloud,

tonal and sonic which here, various as the *icones plantarums*

as they are changing   not in computer-generated hue like any other

a plant that doesn't stand on itself   or observing takes its own "body" and presses it   it may seem

arbitrary but it may be all spandrel   like fiddlehead fern turns their own turning into something

complex and delicate, or stirfried for several minutes delicious with garlic, or a little tough   just as

each brown spot under each leaf carries a plan   with what hue will you excavate me?

a thrill to see your tendrils expand themselves   your outline takes place in tender greys

Apparent Orbits

When time has allowed the stars to drift apart,
a spectral type O reaches a lower temperature

and along the abscissa of the graph maintains
bursts along seams of circles.

If you think music is harmony of spheres
then absolutes placed in the upper left

please those instigated who set margins
measured in luminosity.

The intrinsic brightness does not represent
magnitude, and in your eyes

a telescope, and the same distance,
all their comparisons. If we journey

through the gates of matter correctly,
we enter through the gates of green familiar

and all composition lies open to us
in spectral constellation orbit, tonal.

From Terra, Here

Ownership of the sphere is regrettably inscribed,
as are other particulars with diameters of possession,
as you possess me thus far, and I possess you right back,
all soundwaves and light stop in a digital outpouring,
circular then, about the heart, while time breaks
up into numbers and numbers. Oblivious of delineation,
a volume of air, or a mass of water, while we attend
mutual emptiness, a protractor draws a circle about itself.
An inscription drawn on your back, one finger traces
the amount of vertebrae. We foretell the past
through arrangement of ribs, think of others, even as
we walk over objects left on the ground, half-eaten
things like french fries scattered on water...
In a day saturated with physics, rain falls
with the regularity of years spent guessing events,
a glisson, we slide over a sidewalk broken with omens.
Even as we head uptown, and my hand moves
downward with a knowledge of numbers, our
conclusion hints at an equation laid out earlier in
a watery morning. We count birds out the
window while thinking of empty-headed circles.
It's come round to this: a chance to fill up glasses
with a liquid we wouldn't know was open-hearted.
Solid to the core, light plays over ceilings, spheres
of light as changeable as air blows through
windows. We spend the morning guessing interiors,
believing eyes are doorways, a chance
to scratch names into glass or into each
other's vision. Would you believe a rotation
of spheres lay beyond our range
of perception? Or that through irises are colors
of imagination oceans, a chance to read
outside interiors, circles finding their beginning?

Mars, Naming War

Mars, to you I move naming war
and in my blueness, face with you
our likeness, naming you and in your namesake,
find myself in crimson fields without horizon.
In every cave or earth gray-green, I seek
that for which there is an explanation,
and in explaining find that you are
again next to me in vast expanses.

Your colors flutter across spaces
empty and blue, a splash of crimson
wandering—with darkness at your poles.
Our meteors stumble into gravity
and still with shield, as you are still
with covered face, dust which makes
you as though you were reflective,
our own image in space set
in a frame black as oceans.

We wander crimson without
horizon. You are more and yet
unnamed. We seek in caves
without explanation, inquiring
across expanses, each place
shapes one upon another,
moving through the desert spheres,
find you, Mars, our closest dream of air.

In Jupiter

In Jupiter a room and into rooms,
closet, doorway, and an asteroid orbiting
in bits of ice, rooms, and Jupiter, occupies
a space even as inside that gaseous sphere
a room, and redness beneath delineations
and spun into circulation by gravity
immense, as liquid becomes solid, and
become a denser sphere
definition and occupying a space
as you would push others
into orbits, your circular asteroids
as small planets circle you,
creating space within space as you
take space around yourself and liquid
become gravity, holding yourself
to yourself, to Jupiter, and inside you element
as we would circle you as even gazing
inside you, your core invisible, Jupiter,
you move in and out of visible range,
your largesse and equator, monster.

To Saturn, secure about her rings,
barely visible through a half-moon light,
in an aerial cracking faintly in the turn of things,
things turn in the aether of night against night,
strangely surround roundness accentuated,
in clearness of ancient cataclysm, and marked,
to which you are the only faintness in your turn,
as night would face night, or day comes in cracking,
as he would take telescopes and within the viewpoints
find the neatly fit within and about the magnetic glasses,
through the half-moon lit as though found inside an angle,
a telescope bending and mirrored within,
as astronomer, I, mark the half-cracking night,
as glass ground, or spectacles invented,
would bring the world into clearer focus,
mark the strewn rings of matter,
of matter made, rocks and certain debris,
speaking of a time cataclysm happened
a crackle faint against the half-moon light,
spotlight diffused as though from an angle,
when bounced back and against roundness found,
great round bodies marking matter,
in clarity and turning night against night,
as light would face and in obliqueness,
shatter and mark upon the planet's face day.

To Neptune

Neptune, chaotic you ellipsis ride in obliqueness
and we, unable to predict routes of where
half you disappear and travel as one half
with invisible weight beneath you
as much a boat riding waves unlike your namesake,
becoming as much water as wood and not trident-wielding,
as not bearded water-being half as much water as wood
as gold, as trident enters air from liquid form
as half spun into greenish being and half one with emptiness
as daughters spy through glasses and calculate navigation
not based on your obliqueness, chaotic shell, riding half in darkness
reaching for substance as below you are solitude.

Neptune, you tiny green disk, you faint star,
fainter than distance and as effect your gravity is,
half again more distant in space as you are again distant from us,
when the motion of another did not conform to prediction,
your weight thrown against those within close orbits
as calculations closed in upon your position.
A daughter moved and leaving on shells, with spyglass to eye
seeing distance and again moving in shadows over another,
a demi-circle, a gold half-sphere, as waves rise
and capture objects over them, riding in prediction,
each route you take, captured in equation
marking precisely your green and gold spun orbit
and gravity thrown against others,
half again water and half faint star.

Opticks

In downstairs bathroom, found
drawer of old oak files, plastic
white letters spelling out GOAD
and CEAE, abovefloors behind glass.
XUL SOLAR says "upward,
behind the upstreaming it moored,"
and remembered always outside
correspondences are meant to be
with paper, twine and tape wrap,
and cardboard, cloth, soap and string,
but then found again on the table,
one of those things hinted at, instead
of creating everything from nothing.
The task says K is to surf the waves
of information, and if I am blind in a library
then all directives change to truth.
All is made of trees, letters are found
underneath a cardboard box, a little
orange and on the opposite wall,
a quadrangle of printed letters and papers,
black on white, and after sliding doors
large yellow, four small reds.
E says architecture will be soft, while J
says everything tries to be round.
And writes: Negative I source you see
me a great deal significant in depth.

The Formation of Opticks

mechanicks forme a study the resolution of light
dimmed by beetle infestation miles of thousands of trees
miles of thousands such light must travel even as lifting
across the trees a bare gray line dividing mechanicks
that it's warming cannot be denied if you deny your own
such senses and heat as light lifts and becomes heat and
through atmospheric spaces enters and gives such longer
days and hours and seasons expand as wood sighs and
gives up, lifting of itself into light, as sap sighs and lifts
life, light, as creaks open and reveals itself to sich beetles
as warmer open resolutions study the mechanicks sunne
as you would open yourself and realize sich resolution as light
lifting, from a, I saw you across country as laid waste to,
quarries I see you across and your shadow thrown
timberlines in visible light drawn gray and then green
realization a bare green line must travel as chewing mandibles
past the place in reverie studying the forme that was once there
a forme of shorter seasons and sich snow as laid over mountains
and quarries and timber, snow in longer season as captured light
reflexions and light thrown back into atmospheric spaces

54

The Mechanicks of Formation

explain you I this light and whose equation lies upon
the mountains so flatly and outlined as I you form and
fixed in purpose cast inside the metals and subject as reacted
to formation image resolving such optics as I would settlement
action decision reaction and (a force) component waves break
in a multi-colored delineation upon negation possession in which
exist I you such as comes over forgetting in which place exist
delineation as moving away from such forgetting in place which
exist as goes stretching out and possession oblivion establish
in equation over possession such as mechanicks forme giving
of dissolve form of giving loose and resolve as whether I you
decision reaction darkening under sigh as negation formation
undergo resolution such weakness as overcome cast from light
purpose subject to cast from formation and casting dependent
such depending as needing and coming over and existing
complete name weighing in as such a name exists nothing as weighing
nothing and dissolving in light resolving and flatly outlined
in such existence as you I resolving and forming out of light
multi-colored delineation creeping forward we compositions
of self which light and optics emanate establish outward such
movement optics on hills and valleys such resolution.

botanic

it takes a color to lift eyes
like finding something "pure"
a field of verveine perhaps, if that's possible
if it were, I would write away for it
yellow stretches to the horizon
stretches as if it had started from a concentrated area centralis
in the domesticated breeds, that center of ganglions allows a certain kind of vision
unlike a horizontal "stripe" of nerves better for long-distance hunting
maybe that's what aligns us with the far edge of the horizon
and allows us to see what sort of sea is there
like we know what kind of retina we possess
where our ganglion-bundles are, that might "limit" us
as if we weren't that horizon over the other horizon
writing away from that edge toward another edge
a stripe meeting another stripe
that sense of falling off—or shearing away
a yellow like no other yellow: it's still water
and a plant, pollinating in sunshine
something passes by and throws a shadow

walking stick and enclosed in amber *mecoptera* on isolated
mesa surrounded by desert *phthiraptera* barren what does it
live on small armored *dermaptera* half one thing and half
another *orthoptera* external hard encased *siphonaptera* listening
what distance stripped *strepsiptera* one wondering what it or
it could be one *heteroptera* wingless and vicious sweet *mantodea*
no name for one's own listening *neuroptera* if each were
discovered a radio's long wave *lepidoptera* the beetles and
the termites biting *embioptera* such visibility no major sources
of light pollution urban just eroded spire psire eir *raphidioptera* no
food source and no water ancient pine trees and resin rock slick
psocoptera found within itself others a ravishing *trichoptera* thrips
and book lice *coleoptera* small clouds and visible evaporation scent
megaloptera faults folded thrust ersion rosion sliding *isoptera*
dobsonflies and webspinners *phasmatodea* not one name and another
ephemeroptera dust devils invasive shrubs miles such armor *homoptera*
and what is one and another in mesa in mineral *odonata* silverfish and
jumping bristletails most are plant-eating *hymenoptera* inside one self
eroding salt intrusions slow flexing *blattodea* landscape one and visibility
another rock one you and not what one is, armored *thysanoptera* within
one self another you and rock in mesa surrounded no pollution ution
lusion pol polis *plecoptera* stoneflies, webspinners and mantids,
earwigs, angel wings, cicadas *blattodea* when one thinking they were
gone and in amber discovered one *zoraptera* the gladiator, armored
one who eats others, a carnivore, predator *grylloblattodea* but without
bt wtht to one without wtht a name no name unnamed *diptera* only
the name of others inside one armored the predator others *zygentoma*
archaeognatha on such mesa surrounded by miles long wave radios
listening for pollution, plltn, erosion, rsn, elision, pollus, erode, the
bug listening there on top of the mesa, encased and armored the exo-
skeleton, the fossil, ecout rsion, sliding the name the names
of others inside one and does it live the mantis-walkingstick-
grasshopper predator, carnivore, waiting and ravishment such bare
sand, rock, slick, the *mantophasmatodea*, gladiator, armored, going in.

The Anatomy of Oil

in a room of high round hills
and the room of water cutting
out of reach, the deep rooms
upon rooms, in bands of red,

orange, brown. We drift lower,
thirsty and surrounded by minerals,
the history of that, which:
    that, which leads us to deep
    histories, depths of hunger
    for which there is no resolve:

      As it spreads along the sills impermeable
      in best-intentioned effusion of life,
      teeming, but between intent and discovery,
      a canyon, chasm,
          that is, to explore one seam
          with intent to destroy the next.

      As bodies slowly fall, to fall
      together or one after the other.

        Like islands do, join
        in surface flux, disjointing
        the floating plates *under*
        us (but not written to us),
        us with notebooks in hand.

      Lines extend from continents
      to seas unseen in this chasm.
      Walls block escape and limit
      sky, but here is where
      we thirsty in the seams

liquid with end in sight,
are everywhere around.

It lights our lanterns
and forms our oars.
Over each other in our boat
looking for it climb
in profusion we do,
hungry   as we always are
as we   burn   *it*

       those lines extend from us
       straight from us to the sea
       and ocean floor, perfect
       and simple, over what we
       thought was the end of land—
       giant sea-worms, tubes, mouth-
       less and eyeless, under storm
       of falling life, catching without
       hands, into which
       all bone becomes new skin

treeless in the desert for days
its beauty, inverse to its fertility
      but why call it beautiful? I can't even see it

it's a *national* monument, enclosed within
itself and meant to be seen in a sort
of grouping, a clustering together, a kind
of huddle. Like uranium under quicksand,
it draws us into a kind of state, a hooded
state, it already knew, and within us,
cracking steam, and, on the horizon,

a signal on the top of mountains, a rope
thrown down—we leave hanging, our
hunger, the turn in the river with no exit.

thin soil that, walked on, crumbles away

●○○

Hoodoos and goblins, arsenic and salt springs
petroglyphs and rock houses, a trickle of river
unbordered by green—the red rock comes straight
down to the bank and is dry, as we speed by
in our 4WD wide wheelbased SUV tinted windows
following the RV with self-enclosed toilet, shower
and small venting ribbons, a TV on dashboard, camera—

        but
        it *is* even
        as it is eroded
        and each rain changes
        the depth of the canyons
        and hills melt away

and colors will not be denied
as they reach through glass and cool air.

●○○

One layer over the next and another laid
down over the first and others until all
is lifted up—and as such climbs higher
and creates within itself *voids*

        and within these vast spaces
        skeletons liquid and trapped
        between water and air, mountain
        and valley, held by such light
        and substance and water, as
        evaporation stops, as we
        would evaporate

        and within these vast spaces
        underground, with two slit
        windows facing frontward
        camouflaged behind hill
        one room is used for
        storage (we think) and the
        other room is used for
        experimentation (we think)
        where nothing could be
        held by such substance,
        where evaporate *where it*
        is not where it not is here
        then where is it

           ❍❍❍

one layer over the next and another
creates within itself voids like those
inside, those petrified objects,
heart, stomach, liver, brain, I,
combustible-engined user and allied
with you. You, fossil-fuel burner
and one of us. Us, together in this
single-stroke engined boat because
it is *fast*. Do you think at the end
of this river is food? Maybe we should

                take this path through the woods
                and see which trees filter light
                and what blue heron flies off
                the pond when approached,
                how much we should like to meet
                its eyes, how much to have
                it speak, it, what is it?

and when it leaves a few feathers behind
to be later crystallized into a profit
mineralized and pumped up between it
and another. Distilled, enhanced,
combusted, then it will fit into our
projections, as *convenient* as could be,
is this a *rant*? even as everyone
laughs a little behind their hands—
           a group of people scrape
           cautiously at a seam, pebbles fall from the design
           into a bucket—   but this structure

this eroded fractured volcanic throat and this six-sided
column fluted down the edges this peak over land of rusty
bobble-headed iron drills, thin threads poke into dry hearts—
rock-bottom cheap
it flows but
elsewhere

if gravel could be ground and rock extracted
sand crushed and siphoned, flyaway soil captured
snow and ice melted, rocky beaches compacted, and
beneath the giant thumping machines small drops well
and conglomerate into solid puddles, crushed the conveyor
belt, the ongoing oceanic drop and slide, to recycle,

this smoky place, this fire hanging above nothing, a simple
space between emittance and smokestack, clear and see-
through, a place between flame and metal, fueled and, at night,
glass shields visible from the waters, a quickly changing
reflection, and slow radiance spreads from the piers
in circles, in transforming rivets, slowly under iron.

When sudden flooding
drives us lower past
crushed abyss of uncertain
epoch; from the rims
falls darkly staining
excess, what we
could find more
of better. Our lights

our oars, a mineral
we found in our pockets
this morning and under
the sleeping bags
even as birds cried
like a cathedral above.

O if we had an oar
and needed something
like that, and standing
in water, air takes
from us what
we thought was
soil, instead, it stains
and sits next to us
as one state sits
next to another
and topography
grows flatter and
drier and flatter
and drier.

These lines are simple, perpendicular,
contradictory, extend to the sea
in extension lined with illumination
a shell-less creature with one
foot and phosphorus—
when it falls, as it does, one after
the other, it lines a newly built
floor, and many others come after
to build a newly built floor,
which sags and is heated,

from underneath comes heat,
and is compressed and forms
something close to what we
are looking for, we look more—

what could unmoving parts say
about where this uplift came from
what caused a ship to rise in desert
we pass through, we are speeding
through, we are the middle of 120
miles *without services* if we run
out of gas we are in super-deep shit.
This animal, this beast, lies across
the highway and its claws leave
deep ruts our wheels bounce
and we are trapped in shimmering
light and visions of trucks and
more trucks as they approach
the undulating city of the coastal
plain, *we were someplace and now
we are someplace* that mega-city
to which we are speeding
120 miles and animals line
the highway and all is fenced
it is tottering toward "E"

but it
is, even
colors reach
through glass
and cool air
without
water

trapped between mountain
and valley, unvented, it lifts

What we think is oxidization the sky here
feels at one with benzene and flammable
clouds noxious vapor at lunch
break clouds ignite and spread flaming drops
over school travels insatiable brilliant
appetite radioactive denizens even, as with
us, on this boat, fleeing or *going toward,*
there is a place we have been before

> the copper river valley rises up on either side mines
> shrouded by eastern forests behind the green
> veil a small city and another, they are rooms
> and worn down in every aspect, as every
> aspect takes from us our treasure rocks
> and dog-eared books. If we feel at one
> with explosion, that is something
> quick and sharp, and not the bobble-headed
> drill in the middle of flat plains and
> the fault-and-block system for miles and
> distance and silence, that is not the gradual
> wearing down and the thread poking
> through and the tire treads on crypto-
> organisms turning sand into soil. There are
> warnings here to stay on the trail; there is
> a warning not to go deeper.

> but here we are with
> tiny lanterns, in a canyon

prone to flooding, under
the bright blue lake, blue
against red rocks and the
powerboats singing and
the overpowered jetting,
such transmission, we here
under the blueness, floating
and yet going, a current
almost indecipherable, the
surface unintelligible. It
grows darker as we go,
and around us
all is blue

the substance is not secretive, but untraceable
there are bases but no pyramids
no minarets embedded within missile silos
L-amino acids and DNA dislocated from one to another
pierced by small seeping springs it has wiry leaves
taproots bright white shining purple at a certain hours
at evening, behind the coal-mining operations and over the mesas

◓◒◓

The ships in the thousands in the sea, "he
is doing the bidding of his dark oily masters,"
and the troops think of their children, or so
say the newspapers, the article written about
the woman, his wife, and what she thinks
about the skin rashes, what sort of pills
he eats with breakfast.

The ships by the thousands mass
travelling from here to there and we
in our boat flat-bottomed we wait
for a current, a breeze, "by fear
is the rule of the sea," he holds his crew
with a marble in the palm.

he says each day he gets
information about chemicals
hidden in caves here or
there, our boat floats further
between two walls, on
these walls are inscribed
the news of the day, and
sometimes far up a house
appears, it is inaccessible,
it is uninhabited, we are
not the guardians
of our own history.

They are just stones
falling down one
upon the other, there
is no "we" us here
on this boat and we
what are we but
separate one I you
another over there
no stone fits each
layer different
each other color
red and brown and

orange dark, we are
not we us no we
but then what
is oil? but millions
of creatures crushed
one into another
shoulder
to shoulder

◓◯◑

rising off the river in the morning
that which can no longer be seen
and that which can no longer be said
say: there is
us in this boat and there
are you in your boats, and here
we are under you and you are
above us and you are
against our lanterns, small
circles of light fed by minerals
hungry, for minerals, and minerals
around us, above us, over us
all of us hungry and unintelligible
irreduceable but not traceable
you the same stone and us the same rock
written of us (but not to us)

our boat goes further
between *two walls* and
it grows darker the closer
we come to the mantle

questions: why when the
cavern-structure shifts
geyser blooms blue-orange?
why a horizon of steam evaporates
in columns and perpendicular
wind-blown from bare sand?
why did the mountain town
cover up the vapor caves with
concrete and train tracks? where
do the Utes go now? what rises off
the waters now at this time of day? we
drink everything there is to drink.

Is this the right   *itinerary*? the guides split a while ago
stumbling along the sides of the crevasse,
and now we're trapped like slow-cooling
conglomerate clusters in a lava flow   a petroglyph *there*
where you're *pointing*   more houses higher than any
ladder we have   on top of each hill giving themselves a pleasant
view   as plywood exudes and inhabitants
breathe essence of pulverized forest   each twig
generated by an engine   each section dark
gummy liquid now stuck to our fingers fine webbing as
we feel along in the night for our way unguided

shoulder to shoulder we stand in our way
united and hungry our stomachs are full
we want something and take it from our neighbor
we like it big the next one should be taller
the better to see our land with all the better
to see "our" land to see our "land" the land

73

I love that rock and am amazed at how so large an uplift
can look like a ship, it is the only thing I can think of
to compare to this massive rock *thing* if I could only get
out of the car to take a closer look if only he would
stop and we could climb out of the car and take a closer
look if only the highway would stop and we could climb
out of the car and take a closer look if only the roads
would stop and if only we could look closer at the rock
if only we could stop the car if only we could look

⦿

at it closer if shoulder to
shoulder we stand closer together
but one would not be he
who has had nothing but plenty

a hero, him, who leaves faint marks
on the ground like tracks here
or through the walls lets his hammering
resound, or upstairs, he wears shoes
or checks his mailbox every night
as it swings open to reveal: deep red,
russet, dark brown water-stains, lighter
brownish-gold, bleached, some green,
silvery in contrast. Down the walls
it comes and half the landmark
with it. It's there because we want
it and if we find it we know it is
there and if it's under something
else then that something must

move or be moved and it is poison
in that it is fresh and drops slowly
without acid and small paths lead
to it as we use others to steal it.

In solubility how is water like oil
one is invisible and the other obscure
one combusts and the other is flammable
when one is put into the other it spreads
to where we stand watching how is one
like another how are you liking me how
are you where are you how are we

❍❍❍

Our desert calls to your desert.
Across the earth, one desert speaks
to another, just as water wicks away
into sky. Why so fast? Our desert
is encroaching—we have one, too.
All the world should be a desert.
Because we have a desert, we deny
there is anything beneath it. If you
follow tracks into a hole, you find
a hole. Just like time goes fast on
ultimatums. We translate
rocks to find what's in
between them. Our desert is
not made of sand. Each truck
passes through a small hole.
My hand is the size of a tractor-trailer.
Between my thumb and forefinger,

a truck goes. One truck after another—
so many trucks! What are they shipping?
Dark streaks on the top
of that one, a recumbent
shiny oval. I squeeze it down
to the size of a fire ant. One truck
glows and is closely followed
by another one. Their
routes submerge and resurface
in a giant massing around a
sandy peninsula. At gas stations,
they sleep while underground
fuel tanks regenerate themselves.
My hand is the size of several
axles and slips on ice. The more axles,
the better. If I press here, my headache
goes away and fossil fuel comes out.
I buy vegetables at corner markets
and support the food wax industry.
Each apple shines like black ice. Our
apartment stinks like steam
cracking through soil. Below ground
pipes carry oil for an entire city
in the shadows of forward-leaning
ranges. Each pass harbors
a collection of movie cinemas.
The white truck glides
through traffic and belches black
smoke over people on the sidewalks.
We lean over the sides of our truck
and cast hooks at everything with
rivets in its sides. We ran out of
water a long time ago.

❍❍❍

field lights piled upon each other
illuminating nothing but another field
and after that more fields until a desert
abruptly with sand ends the endless *pré*

it's luminous far beyond the sinking light
all that rises and casts long darkness
from either side of the cañon
for us, sun for only a few hours, for us we

need to light the path and with what
to light the walls? And how to light
the waters on all sides, this timed
sliver of day above, so quickly it turns

dark, that with darkness we counteract,
with dark substance we create a glow,
all it illuminates, past the cañon walls,
and reaching those, find another field

and in that hour which you promised
and which he promised several hours
and days ago, the high tables of land,
the generous wooded hills, the marshy

in-between lands, the sculpted flowers
hanging off the submerged cedars.
To plan certain mist, it is surprising
to exit such dunes stretching away

and find a heavy fog hiding the road.
A small path skirting headlands,
to see such cloud of lights entering
water hissing after so many days

without water or light. Is our hunger
justified? Do dry winds spin faster
over land flattened in the last
glacial event? Will our house be lifted

and deposited in a till of glacial debris,
a giant moraine, a deep bedrock dictating
height, an island formed purely from
the garbage of others. It's the sort

of juice that increases thirst. Electrolytes
know not which way to go. It's pure
salt and a small sign obscures this arsenic
spring. Or the sky ignites from someone's

carelessly dropped corporate exemption.
Follow the dried-out shrub and you'll
find pools of sandy mineral aspiration
at which each animal gathers, excluding

ourselves: we like to have it just for us.
But, did it leave footprints in the water?
Could we find it again if we followed each
branch pointing upward to the flammable crown?

Did this loser hang painted leaves in
each tree, thinking the birds would be misled
into building nests of bendy straws and
tinselly metal threads? Maybe a bolt

or two, but not the entire dumped car,
rusting in the front yard, or where it
rolled down the hill one night, coming
to rest against a large maple tree, just

on the edge of changing, each leaf
a reflection of the same colors displayed
when the prairie is accidentally worn away,
when one small creek grinds down to

the banded deposits below—dusty and
harboring many different kinds of
wildlife, invisible mostly to you and me,
except in that huge space where no

where it's just space, kind of, and
turrets poking into horizon, that's
the closest we could come to drinking
water and driving as quickly as we

could through juniper scent and over
ground beneath us that contains nothing,
nothing! nothing! dust and slight coloration
a bit of iron no interior lights no darkness

The Clocktower

When I saw the clocktower it was an invisible space within.
My eyes ceased to be organs of communication and instead
        became organs of vision.

When I heard bells each hour, but only after childhood in my "tweens"
        between childhood and adulthood, assisted by bells
When the space had been filled in. Empty rooms painted, windows shrunk and lifted up walls.
        The original building grows upward from brick and cast iron. Cast iron over wood, or in
        place of wood. Wood as frames, or something concrete could be poured about. Concrete
        taking the shape and exterior texture of wood. (But never color.)

Color as something defining and stringing along, a medium of communication between us and
        object. Not color-blind. Blinded by color.

Assisted by bells the next character enters. Even before it was invented he was here with the
clocktower. From cast-iron and wood to foot and bolt. From brass and oil to interlocking gears and
concrete filling gaps between splintered wood and brick, terracotta falls from ceiling, creating dust
in its wake. Dust to get into gears and he oils it away again.

Many blank spaces that area materials filled before my eyes in colors: red, gray, and brown. What
color is wood? Wood-colored.

Blank spaces explain to us and as they explain the spaces begin to move.

The question was whether the movement was ahead or around. His work was linear *and* circular.
He had been living with the clock for a long time. Someone leaned against the clockface and left a
small broken circle—a circle of lines and tears, bulging outward over the street. He called the mark
"Kim's passion." The movie star had leaned against it while filming a sex scene.

Red, gray, and brown, with a million variations in between. In my "tweens" I had left bells there.

The roof opens up into a vista. A small elevator and stairway and another stairway open up onto a
roof into a vista. Buildings that had crowded and oppressed on the street become a range,
a skyline, openings, almost decoration, even the ones that were gone. The blank space
becomes a blank space again before it gets filled in. *Filled in* as though it requires a
preposition and an object. But that is what color is about. Color requires an object.

There is duration and after that an object. Whether you last through the duration is the test of the
movie star. It senses what you are about to do and duplicates it before you do it. Before
you achieve it. That is the nature of production.

Production: You work or walk toward the object while seeing it become before you. Walls raise up
and carve themselves out of heavy quarry rock while retaining glittering chips. The chips
fool you into thinking you are wealthy. There is a "pod"—a pod-like shape caught between
layers; it rises up and within itself warps. While also leaving a small space, a void, sort of,
for you to discover.

Once I've discovered it, so does everyone else. So I dynamite it to keep it a secret. Thanks to
somebody else who told me about it. The movie star.

My body blocks the entranceway so they can't get to my trapped foot.

My foot is buried by the rocks I exploded. Out of the way. It was distracting to be the focus of so
many eyes. Camera after camera after camera. And then I went to prison. Or I stayed in
the cave where I was found. If I were found by many. And gazed. Something reflected in
my eyes. A long underground—

I set the explosion and then suddenly I am a focus. Camera after camera— I obliged them to redo
the security protocols. My code name is _____.

Length provides balance. Equilibrium. The hollow circular spots break up my silhouette. No outline
against the peaks.

When I have turned invisible, my eyes cease to see and instead become organs of communication. Only the eyes are left after transparency occurs in sheets.

Only the back of me is reflective. Only heat makes me glisten as though assuming shape in the form of a *rosette*. The rosettes break up the image so that I become invisible against rocks. As though assuming shape is another function of color. Color is demanding. Color takes over. An avalanche—what color? What form!

The rosettes collapse against rock ages old. Tracks left around the recording machines even as voices make smartass remarks and think they are involved in the recording. They are *displaying* their role in the movie. Even when their lungs burst and they are carried back down to the film studios.

If I remembered the roof. Overlooking the streets and dams and rivers of childhood. There was the building where it all happened. Cornices drop off like tears. Warning after warning that rusting and falling, iron falling off hitting, top of head hit, falling off. There was that street. A little bit of reproaching, of recycling. On the roof being recycled. Draped over the clockface. Showering on the clockface or on the roof, draped in linens. Hidden by shades or by windows. A windowshade to block progression as blank spaces move. Can only see the tops of trees. The little tops of trees.

The next character enters. He remembers as memory is encapsulated within building. A small twig placed against rosettes. As the animal carries the twig up to the roof. A leaf or small twig captured in the gutter. A thread with a small rosette of wear in a kink—an explosion of fray, wrapped around the leaf, signalling it. Suspending it above the gutter in a structure of leaf, thread—both worn, becoming brittle and fractionalizing.

The next character enters: a *rastaquouère*. Living in a grand space. When spaces are rare. A giant space elsewhere that resists being populated. A nostalgia for fray. His eyeglasses reflect the half-floors and dusty light and unfinished floors recording traces. Filming it, discovers shadows. Shadows are what comprise a decent film. One that keeps you up until 4 a.m. or is a matinee. Like matinees exist anymore. Like anyone knows the time during the day without a public clock.

That's what kept me going between the cast iron and the subway station. Between childhood and adolescence. A good movie at 4 a.m., comprised of shadows. And the public clock in the subway station.

A clock is good for keeping one going. The second hand sweeps all there is before it. Even as the rush of air signals a train moving forward. The train arrives with the new minute. As the second hand foretold.

It returns to hands. The index finger being smaller than the ring finger or roughly the same size. It was a way to measure it. It was time to get down. Someone else researched it. For me.

And then it became true. As like wood. It was patterned after the molding devices used to put it into place. They—who? Poured it in and made it conform. It was like there was no time. The bridge took place slowly, almost by itself. I saw it down the street at half mast, then becoming itself. It plunged into water and became half-bridge, half-liquid.

Delicate—I had assumed it was rough and wild. As things observed often are. It stalked my cameras and undid the microphone so slowly static was indiscernable from language.

Funny how construction occurs outside time and place. I pick up again where I first experienced it. I am older and I am busy. Rosettes take place and break up the image, leaving static where a body stalked. Here is the rock he/me/it stepped on; here is the print. Or it spoke here. Opened its lips and said … maybe the hour or minute. Only a trace, or an afterimage, a breath against rock or cornice or the first step of a long stairway, or the spinning wheels of an elevator. Changing the grease and oil and polishing the cups. Window holds a fingerprint as painting takes place under the ceiling. Painting and then some kind of crank, pulling up. Floors replicate and add on windows, framed and then catching perspective as height takes over. Here is the party on the roof: here are the bodies, some disappearing over edges, here is the performance piece and the man hanging off the roof, here is the music evaporating toward the horizon. Here is the tour later; the recording devices. Here are the visitors, trying to *envision* change and later, what happened. The cave collapsed, the foot was crushed, the image coalesced. Turn eyes toward me, translucence swiftly rises. Why the building here and then the clock within it. Solid, straight, and always on time. As bells ring, and then stop, and start again—funding dries up, and comes back, and stops again. Color within its medium. Whether transmitted or transformed. Whether eyes communicate or register. As I delicately choose to paint which piece visible, with color. For me. A rosette for the characters one used to be.

Many deep thanks to Rachel Levitsky, Erica Kaufman, Lytle Shaw, Daniel Bouchard, and as ever, to Richard O'Russa, who reads where it begins. Thank you also to the editors of *The @ttached Document*, *Aufgabe*, *The Denver Quarterly*, Dolphin Press, durationpress.com, fauxpress.com, *GAM*, *The Germ*, *Insurance*, *The Ixnay Reader*, *POeP!*, *Primary Writing*, *Rattapallax*, *The Recluse*, *Sal Mimeo*, and Web del Sol, for publishing poems from *Area*.

For my mother and father.

"an aggravated shape" is a collaboration with O'Russa and was shown at the Lower Manhattan Cultural Council's Small Works exhibition as part of the 2005-2006 residency program.

"The Orange Line" was developed as a collaborative scroll with O'Russa and performed at the the 2007 New Year's Day Marathon at the Poetry Project at St. Mark's Church.

"Scale Shift" appeared in the anthology *Whitman Hom(m)age, 2005/1885*, published jointly by Turtle Point Press, New York, and Joca Seria in Nantes, France, 2005. Excerpts from "Scale Shift" will be included in 2009 in an outdoor pathway for the East Village Multipurpose Center for Senior Citizens at Van Nuys Sherman Oaks Park in California, as part of a project by artist Hillary Mushkin.

The poem "False Color View" was written for a reading in May 2004 at the Drawing Center in New York City to accompany the show *Ocean Flowers: Impressions from Nature*. That poem, along with the series "Remote Sensing" and "The Verneuil Process," were inspired by the process of how visual images of natural phenomena are manipulated, from Victorian-era naturalists pressing pigmented plants into paper to contemporary scientists enhancing the color and contrast of images of planets, nebulae, and other phenomena. The Verneuil Process refers to how artifical rubies are made.

"The Apparent Orbits" was published as a series in *The Ixnay Reader*. Earlier versions were published as part of an e-chapbook, "The Body, Light, and Solar Poems," on durationpress.com. "Neptune" was printed as a letterpress broadside by Dolphin Press, New Lights Press, Maryland Institute College of Art. Poems from Apparent Orbits were presented at the Inspiration of Astronomical Phenomena Conference at the Adler Planetarium in Chicago, IL, in 2005. Some seed material comes from *Exploring the Planets*, by Iain Nicholson, No. 42, *Stars, Planets, and Galaxies*, by Sune Engelbrektson, No. 54, of the Knowledge Through Color series published by Bantam Books, 1971; and *Notebooks of Leonardo da Vinci*, Dover, 1970.

"botanic" accompanied Zachary Wollard's painting "Trans-Siberian Express" in his 2005 catalogue.

"The Anatomy of Oil" was published as a letterpress chapbook by Belladonna Books in 2005.

Marcella Durand's books include *Traffic & Weather*, *The Anatomy of Oil*, *Western Capital Rhapsodies*, *City of Ports*, and *Lapsus Linguae*. Her poems and essays on the intersections of poetry with ecology, architecture, and art have appeared in *Conjunctions*, *NYFA Current*, *Ecopoetics*, *26*, *Chain*, and other journals. She was a writer-in-residence at the Lower Manhattan Cultural Council in 2006, and in 2005, organized a reading and panel on the inter-relations between astronomy and poetry as part of the Inspiration of Astronomical Phenomena Conference at the Adler Planetarium in Chicago. For the past several years, she has been translating Michèle Métail's book-length work, *Les horizons du sol/Earth's Horizons*, a history of the geological formation of Marseille written within an Oulipian formal constraint. She has lived in NYC more or less since she was small, with interludes in Boston, New Orleans, Cork, Ireland, and Paris, France. She currently lives in the East Village with her husband Richard O'Russa and son Ismael Toussaint Durand O'Russa.

Colophon

Area was printed in a first edition of 1000 copies by Thomson-Shore, Inc on acid free Natures Natural, 50% post-consumer recycled paper. Printed in the United States, 2008.

The interior of *Area* was typeset in Calson and Helvetica, and the cover is set Bookman Old Style and Gill Sans.

The front cover of *Area* features original artwork © Suzan Frecon.
    purple forbidden enclosure
    oil on linen
    87 $^3/_8$ x 108 inches
    2005

Also By Belladonna Books

Four From Japan
Contemporary Poetry & Essays by Women
edited by Sawako Nakayasu
(published in collaboration with Litmus Press)

Open Box
Carla Harryman

Mauve Sea-Orchids
Lila Zemborain
translated by Rosa Alcalá and Mónica de la Torre